Shopping Ad[diction]
Effective Tactics to He[lp...]
Buying an[d...]

Emily V. Steinhauser

Gamma Mouse
www.gammamouse.com

SHOPPING ADDICTION BOOT CAMP
Copyright © 2014 by Emily V. Steinhauser.
All rights reserved.

First Edition: May 2014
1234567890
A Gamma Mouse eBook
Published by Gamma Mouse, a dba of Xilytics, LLC.
www.gammamouse.com

This document is geared towards providing exact and reliable information in regards to the topic and issue covered. The publication is sold with the idea that the publisher is not required to render accounting, officially permitted, or otherwise, qualified services. If advice is necessary, legal or professional, a practiced individual in the profession should be ordered.

From a Declaration of Principles which was accepted and approved equally by a Committee of the American Bar Association and a Committee of Publishers and Associations.

In no way is it legal to reproduce, duplicate, or transmit any part of this document in either electronic means or in printed format. Recording of this publication is strictly prohibited and any storage of this document is not allowed unless with written permission from the publisher. All rights reserved.

The information provided herein is stated to be truthful and consistent, in that any liability, in terms of inattention or otherwise, by any usage or abuse of any policies, processes, or directions contained within is the solitary and utter responsibility of the recipient reader. Under no circumstances will any legal responsibility or blame be held against the publisher for any reparation, damages, or monetary loss due to the information herein, either directly or indirectly.

Respective authors own all copyrights not held by the publisher.

The information herein is offered for informational purposes solely, and is universal as so. The presentation of the information is without contract or any type of guarantee assurance.

The trademarks that are used are without any consent, and the publication of the trademark is without permission or backing by the trademark owner. All trademarks and brands within this book are for clarifying purposes only and are the owned by the owners themselves, not affiliated with this document.

Acknowledgements

I would like to thank my wonderful Mom and Dad who instilled in me the love to help people live happier and healthier lives.

And to my husband, Paul, who puts up with me researching and writing at the strangest hours.

Introduction

It has definitely happened to the best of all – going shopping on an idle Sunday for a formal white shirt for an upcoming important presentation at the office, and after a two hour frenzy, ending up with two whole new ensemble; complete with matching scarves, bags, shoes and even makeup.

Or, getting the paycheck for the month and deciding to do a little window shopping for yourself, perhaps treating yourself to a scarf or a sensible pair of shoes; but ending up with not only spending the whole month's salary, but overdrawing your bank balance, wondering how to pay the rent for the rest of the month, or what to spend on groceries and cab fare?

As I said before, this has happened to all of us at one point of our time or other. Once or twice, even thrice in a lifetime – that's fine! Mistake made, lesson learned – that's fine, too! But what if this is the regular scene that you witness every week, every month, year after year? What if your finances are a mess because it seems like you're constantly buying one thing or another?

When you open your already stuffed closet to stuff these unwanted and unnecessary purchases into it, do these questions come to your mind?

"When did I buy this T-shirt? What was I thinking?"

"I don't wear this color! Why did I buy this dress?"

"Do these shoes even fit me? When did I get them?"

"What am I going to do with these pants? I don't think I will ever wear them!"

"Why do I have all these clothes? Why do I keep on buying things I'll never ever wear?"

It looks to me like you have a slight problem, isn't that so?

Limited Time Free Offer

Download the #1 Bestseller from Gamma Mouse Media for FREE! Hurry this offer won't last as it is for a limited time only. Reserve your free copy today at http://gammamouse.com.

Understanding Shopping Addiction

That problem that is hampering your life is a disorder known as Shopping disorder or Oniomania – the compulsive desire to shop; most commonly known as shopaholism, shopping addiction, compulsive shopping or Compulsive Buying Disorder, or CBD.

The Compulsive need to shop – it's not such an uncommon tendency among people. More or less everyone in this world is a fan of spending their money for shopping, whether it is designer clothes, electronic gadgets, books, jewelry or for a lucky handful – cars. However, when this shopping spree becomes an addiction and you are crossing your limits to purchase things that you do not need or cannot afford, and in turn ruining your finances, is when this becomes a disorder.

Shopping disorder may not be as dangerous as alcoholism, or drug abuse, or even hoarding or kleptomania, but sometimes, it can be as destructive and vicious as the above mentioned. People with shopping disorders are always putting their future, and their families', in jeopardy as they go on spending their money in an irresponsible and careless manner, money that should have been used for other important purposes.

Shopping disorder is seen relatively more among women than men; and they are more prone to spend money than their male counterparts. In the United States, around 5.8% of the total population can be said to be seriously affected by compulsive buying.

Compulsive buying can be considered a shopping spree on impulse, an obsessive compulsive disorder, an addiction or a clinical disorder. It certainly does enough damages to a person's lifestyle to be called a dangerous addiction. Shopaholism has the power to destroy families, relationships, friendships and careers. People get into such financial distress which takes them years to recover from.

In those terms, perhaps compulsive shopping disorders can be termed almost as dangerous as any other mental disorders.

It is true that at today's age of commercialism, the average person always ends up buying a little more than everything that they might need. However, for the average person, this excess is only in terms of three dresses when you need one, ten pair of shoes when four pairs would have been enough, a slightly bigger TV or the latest Smartphone released this week.

Going overboard is when you end up with fifty dresses, a hundred pair of shoes, a separate TV for every room in your house, and when you are juggling four Smartphone when a person can just need one. This may be normal when you are an heiress or a multi-millionaire in the making, but for the average Joe, this habit will certainly break a person's wallet, and their bank balance.

Almost anyone - from any age, gender and background – is in risk for shopping addiction.

However, this disorder is more seen among teenagers and people in their early 20s. This is because this is the perfect time when a person gets their own bank accounts, their own money, and their own credit cards, and makes a sudden transition from pocket money to earnings. This is when they stop being independent on their parents for money or for guidance regarding shopping, and get an opportunity to spend on their own.

Recognizing a Compulsive Buyer

It's not hard to recognize a person who shops to meet their needs and a person who needs to shop without actually having the need for anything at that point. A shopaholic's signs are precise and easily noticeable.

Ignoring the Budget

We are all fond of nice things, and many of us like to spend our hard earned cash in the pursuit of the latest gadgets or our favorite designer's hottest collection. Most of us allot a monthly budget to be spend on these 'extras', and there may be a few times that we cross that budget.

A person with shopping disorder, however, will completely ignore the budget every single time. They might make a budget before they set out to shop, but very conveniently forget all about it when they begin.

Besides, a normal person, when they like something that is more expensive than they can afford, might say something like, "Too bad! I can't afford that" and put it back. A person with shopping disorder will not acknowledge the budget or the fact that they are crossing the boundaries of their budget by buying that particular thing.

Obsessive Behavior

A person with a shopping disorder is usually driven by impulse. He or she may purchase four or five items of a product when they didn't even need one, without even sparing a thought. Sometimes, a women may enter into a shop meaning to buy one pair of shoes for an occasion, and coming out with five or six others, sometimes even with matching bags – and other items that they didn't need, didn't plan to buy, or have no use of. They hadn't thought about the reason of the purchase while they were buying them, and instead bought them on a whim.

This is seen more when they are on a spree to buy birthday presents, or Christmas gifts. They go into the shop to buy somebody a birthday present, and end up buying presents for everybody in the family, or in the office – though it is neither their birthdays, nor did they need anything. On Christmases, they tend to buy multiple gifts for the same person without even stopping to think of the reason or of their finances.

Persistent Problem

While it is common for an average person to slip up once or twice and e swept away with designer boutiques and latest fashions, it is a chronic problem for someone who suffers from shopaholism. They will repeat the same patterns day after day, month after month, year after year. For them, it's not only the holiday season, or anyone's birthday, or shopping for a special event – a shopaholic will spend and waste money buying unnecessary things they didn't need and they will never use.

It's not that a sufferer of compulsive shopping doesn't try to stop their habit, but days turn into months and into years before they can actually take a stand against themselves; and with passing time, their addiction only grows stronger.

Vicious Circle of Shopping

Unlike many other disorders, a person with compulsive shopping disorder sometimes knows when they have crossed the lines. This is usually the time when they come face to face with a credit card bill, or an empty wallet, or when they are unable to makes ends meet the rest of the month because they have spent all their wages.

This is when the sufferer is overcome with shame and guilt. Sometimes, they take back their purchases for refund to the shops. However, compulsive buying runs in a vicious circle, and more often than not, the sufferers are seen to have bought more than they had come back to return; thus creating a vicious circle around them.

In some cases, sufferers of CBD try to ease the guilt of shopping through more shopping, getting into more financial trouble than before. Like a person with an eating disorder or an alcoholic, they try to appease their guilt and shame and initiating another shopping spree.

Concealing the Problem

It is very rare for a person with shopping disorder to come clean about their habits, although it is their own earnings that they spend and they are not answerable to anyone. However, most shopaholics tend to lie about and hide their purchases, since they are afraid others will criticize them.

This problem affects women more than men; they often deceive their husbands or their partners about their financial situations and their activities. In many cases, marriages end in divorce and relationships fail because of such matters.

Shopaholics lie and conceal because they are fearful of other's criticisms, their anger, and most importantly, because they themselves feel guilty and ashamed of their actions.

Preoccupation with Shopping

A shopaholic will spend a major part of their day thinking about shopping and spending. If they are not shopping at the moment, they will be thinking about going shopping, planning on what to buy, thinking of ways to manage money, or looking through magazines for sales and discounts. In all – all their thoughts and plans will be regarding heading off to the nearest shop and spend.

If some of the character traits above seem familiar to you, we have a list of questions that will definitely help you to tell whether a person has a problem, or is just an enthusiastic shopper.

Do you always buy the things you want, without thinking whether you need it or you can afford it?

Do you go shopping when you're angry, sad, excited or think you deserve a treat?

Do you spend almost all your money immediately after you get your wage, or the household money, on things that you would like to buy, not for your home or your family?

Does almost one-third, or more, of your income or spending money go into paying your personal bills?

Do you lie about your spending or your personal bills to your family and friends?

Do you buy multiple numbers of your favorite things, such as your favorite perfume, jewelry or makeup before they are used up; or stack up on more gadgets or books before you have used the previous ones?

Are you always juggling your finances and your lifestyle?

Do you try to ease your guilt of spending with more shopping?

Are you always crossing the budget you make for yourself?

Do you lose control of yourself when you begin shopping?

If you answer affirmative to as many as five of these question, you – or the friend or family that you are seeking these answers for - might have Compulsive Buying Disorder, or CBD. You should seek help immediately.

How Shopping Disorder can harm you

Shopping disorders may not be as dangerous as alcoholism or substance abuse, but it still has the power to turn your life upside down. This disorder can have an effect in almost all sides of your life, and can destroy relationships, careers and everything that you hold dear and everything that you have worked for in life.

Effect on Finances

Probably, a person's finances suffer the most from this disorder, both in the form of wages spent or credit cards overdrawn. Since a person with shopping disorder seldom stays within a budget, very often they spend almost all of their wages the moment they get their monthly or weekly salary. They are incapable of stopping at one point of purchasing to think about what to use for grocery, rent or bills for the rest of the days of the month/week.

When all the cash is used up, an addict usually reverts to borrowing from friends, family and colleagues; almost always they fail to pay them back. If sometimes they had the cash available to pay back what they owe others, they prefer to spend it up instead of paying. Therefore, besides having very little to spend on their homes and families, shopping addicts generally owe a large amount of money to others.

Besides, wives and partners have been known to spend money from joint accounts without consulting their husbands or significant others, only to be caught red-handed when the bills arrive. Joint accounts which are kept aside for emergencies or just for groceries and household products are spent for their personal purchases or for paying their personal bills.

Addicts are known to have spent the amount kept aside for mortgage or for children's tuition fees or even some much needed medical emergency on clothes, shoes or gears. It is not unheard of cases when a husband or a wife has spent money that had been saved for someone's medical bills or a much needed surgery.

Perhaps the most dangerous case is when a person suffering from Compulsive buying Disorder, when out of cash to spend, turns to their credit cards. Sopping addicts generally carry a number of credit cards, sometimes more than five or six, each of them overdrawn and reaching the maximum amount. They never seem to come around to pay back the amount they owe to the banks, satisfied with only paying back the minimum amount or the interest amount at most. Often, instead of paying their minimum amount, they even pretend not to have received the bill or reminders from banks, throwing them away or not taking notice of them. They tend to completely ignore the matter entirely until they end up owing thousands of dollars to the bank, without any way of paying it back.

Effect on Relationships

Spending and shopping disorders have a very negative effect on relationships and families, too. Marriages break up and families are destroyed due to this habit of someone.

People with shopping disorders tend to lie a lot; they lie about their purchases, about their finances, about the nature of their spending. Sometimes spouses spend the money they had for their household expenditure on their personal shopping sprees and never tell the other one, until caught red-handed when the bills come home. Significant others use up the amount in their joint account without consulting the other one.

In many marriages, husbands or wives threaten their partner with divorce unless they stop shopping. However, as with all other disorders, stopping is hard and the matter is often dragged to divorce. Families break up as children watch their parents behave irresponsibly regarding their finances, spending their college tuition on personal extravagant items.

People with this disorder are generally pre-occupied with only one thought – shopping! They prefer to go out and spend money rather than spend time with their family and friends. They are often anxious and jumpy, and become defensive and cranky if someone interrogates them about their shopping.

Friends are estranged because addicts have no time to spend with them. They lie and cheat, and always seek to borrow money – pushing friends away from themselves.

Effect on Emotions

People with shopping disorders are generally emotionally drained, always anxious and are constantly having mood swings. Shopping always gives them a rush and a surge of uncontrollable happiness, but that joy is very short-lived. Almost immediately they are filled with shame and guilt, which they try to wash away with even more shopping.

Shopping addicts are always pre-occupied with spending and buying. They are of a nervous and jumpy nature; lying and deceiving comes second nature to them. They are always misleading others with made up stories and lies to cover their habits or their spending. They become defensive and hostile if anybody confronts them.

Addicts put shopping habits before their family and friends, and begin to alienate people. They go on shopping but are never satisfied with their purchases. They seldom use the items they buy for themselves; but instead, they end up hoarding them or giving them away.

Effect on Health

To some extent, shopping disorder has an inverse effect of a person's health. Anxiety and worrying are commonly seen in a person who is addicted to shopping. They are constantly living on the edge; they feel overexcited and fanatic during a sale or closing time. They are sometimes reckless drivers and irresponsible on the streets, and in their eagerness to reach a shopping mall or a sale, cause accidents.

Besides, when a person who has shopping disorder is unable to indulge themselves in shopping – due to a credit card being maxed out or having been threatened by a spouse or family – diverts themselves towards other bad habits that may be harmful to their health. Eating disorders are a common practice among shopaholics who are trying to recover or control themselves. Smoking and drinking habits also appear.

Effect on Career

Careers are sometimes put at risk for a person who is addicted to shopping and buying. Employees in important designations are known to take long lunch breaks, take off early from work or even take a day off because they had to attend a sample sale or a special discount. They forget about important meetings they had to attend, important presentation they had to prepare for or special clients they had to be attentive to because they were pre-occupied with shopping.

It is not unheard of that employees had been fired as they were caught red-handed, multiple times, browsing an online shopping website when they were supposed to be working on a report, or cruising the malls on the pretense of visiting a client.

The effects of shopping disorder may not be life-threatening as of some other disorders, but it certainly has enough power to destroy one's life.

Treatment Options for Shopaholics

The options to seek treatment for a shopaholic are many, once they decide that enough is enough and they need to stop. This happens often when the person finds themselves bankrupt or being threatened by their bank. They may recover temporarily, stop spending and get their life back on track with a little effort, but they are very likely to relapse into their old habits soon.

When a person is adamant that they do want to stop their addiction with shopping, there are a few treatment options open for them.

Behavioral Therapy

In this form of therapy, a trained counselor will attempt to change a person's negative shopping behaviors into positive ones. That is, when an addict feels the irrepressible desire to shop, they are taught to direct this desire into some other action that wouldn't harm them.

For example, when a person is in a shopping mall and feels like they have to go into a store, they are instead directed towards the theater where they can spend their time without buying anything. Again, when are bored and have nothing to do, instead of going out for a stroll to the nearest shopping mall, they are taught to redirect their attention to visit their family, call their friends or go for a run.

Cognitive Therapy

In this form of treatment, the counselor – instead of targeting the shopping behaviors of a person – will target their thought patterns. They will change the thoughts of that person so that they stop thinking about shopping and spending all the time, but rather focus positively on the other aspects of their lives – their families, friends, career and health.

This type of therapy has proved to be quite successful, according to the *Journal of Clinical Psychology and Psychotherapy.*

Financial Counseling

When a person with shopping disorder is completely lost and confused with their financial situations, a counselor who is experienced in finance can help. They will go through the person's wages, expenditure and assets in a systematic manner and help set up a budget which tells them exactly how much they can afford to spend on frivolity after paying their rent, bills, food, fare and most importantly, after paying back the banks.

This is often a necessary step for shopaholics who go overboard their budget and never know when to stop spending.

Group Therapy

In group therapy, shopaholics gather together to talk about their problems and their situations in life, especially the negative effects shopping has left in their lives and how they are suffering from it. These gatherings are generally known as 'Shopaholics Anonymous' or 'SA' and are available in every area.

Group therapies keep a keen eye on its members. They actively keep track of its member's spending and other activities; they even call on interventions if the members relapse back on their habits. Regular members within a specific group often become very close to each other and together, they try to limit their expenditures in the occasions that they actually need to go to a mall or departmental store.

Meditation

In many cases, uncontrollable shopping is often a result of hidden depression, anxiety or other disorders in a person. Therefore, meditations that are effective for these symptoms can also be prescribed for shopping disorder. Especially, antidepressants are often prescribed for recovering shopaholics.

However, this is not a popular practice, and not welcome widely.

Self-Help is the Best Help

Of all the treatments of shopping disorder, self-help is still the best path to choose. When a person truly believes that they have a problem and truly wants a way out from the chaotic and haphazard lifestyle that they had created for themselves, solution is possible.

So, if you think that you may have a problem with excessive shopping, or if you have a friend or a family member who needs help, the perfect time to start is RIGHT NOW! We have a few tips for you that will help you on your way to your recovery.

Tip#1: Acknowledge the Problem

The first step to recovering from shopping disorders, as with any other disorder, is to acknowledge and confront your problem. For most people, this happens when, after years of spending and shopping extremely, they have finally come to the point that they have literally ruined themselves. Usually all their savings are gone, all their credit cards maxed out, all their friends and family borrowed from, and their room and closet to the limit of bursting out.

However, it is never too late to start, no matter how much trouble you are in. The moment you stop in your tracks and decide that you have had enough of the 'living dangerously' and hiding from the banks and creditors is the first stage of your recovery.

Tip#2: Look within Yourself

It is a good idea to go back to the root of the problem. Ask yourself: why do I shop? Why do I find shopping so exciting? Am I trying to compensate something in my life through shopping? Why do I get such a thrill when I shop? What is it about this particular hobby that attracts me? Is it the buying, the acquiring of pretty things, or is it the spending?

When you get to the bottom of the problem, the answer may come as a surprise to you. You may discover some problem deeply rooted inside you that you haven't thought about for a long, long time. Or, it may not even be a problem; it may be that you enjoy shopping just for the sake of it. If that is the matter, it may be easier for you to distract yourself towards another hobby.

Tip#3: Stick to the List

Shopping is something that cannot be avoided no matter what. You will need to shop for groceries, presents and even for clothes at one time. As a recovering shopping addict, the first time you venture out to the malls and stores may prove to be difficult for you.

Make an occasion of it. For grocery shopping, go to the departmental store once a week. Make a list of everything that you will need throughout the week and STICK TO IT. If that means 7 apples and 7 frozen dinners, then take only 7 and no more. Don't make it 8 thinking of accidents or company or anything else. Do not buy a single item outside the list even if there's a massive sale going on.

When you are out buying clothes, be very specific in your needs. Make a list in this case too. "I have a Christmas office party coming on and I need a new ensemble. 1 dress, 1 stocking and 1 pair of black shoes." Be very specific; make that 'a short black formal dress within XXX dollars, simple black stocking to go with the dress and 1 pair of black heels within XXX dollars'. Most importantly, don't end up buying a purse just because it would look great with the dress and the shoes, or because it was a great bargain. No matter how much of a discount you would have got, you have to stick to the list.

Tip#4: Pay with what you have

Pay with cash, always. With cash, you will always know your limits, and know exactly how much you have left to go through the rest of the month. Checks and debit cards are also fine as long as you are keeping track of how much you are spending and how much you have left in your account.

Avoid Credit cards completely. Throw away or cut off all your credit cards and keep only one for emergencies. Remember, emergencies are only accidents, helping out family and friends, and illnesses.

Sales, discounts and deals are not emergencies and neither are holidays, treating yourself or a pair of shoes.

While spending with credit cards, people feel like they don't need to return that amount to the banks. Since spending with credit cards is not spending hard-earned money, the amount spend doesn't seem real. People usually end up much more than they intended to spend, since they are not spending money out of their own pockets.

In short, use the money you earned and you have, and you can never overstep the boundaries of your budget.

Tip#5: Avoid Temptation

Avoid any place that might tempt you. This can be the shopping mall, department stores, even farmer's markets and street markets. Don't go to these places until you have a list of things that actually need to buy for yourself or your home. If you need to look for a place to hang out or have time to kill, head to the local park or catch a movie.

Stop flicking through shopping channels and reaching for the phone. Avoid visiting online shopping websites while browsing the internet. A lot of unnecessary shopping happens this way.

If you still need to go to a mall, don't 'shop'; instead, 'window shop'. If you see something that you feel like you 'just have to have', write it down on your list. Wait for a few days and if you still feel like you need it, go for it. Try to fit it in your budget and your list for the next week/month. There's no harm in treating yourself now and then, as long as you can stay within your visit.

Tip#6: Set your Priorities

Your first priority as a recovering shopaholic should be to pay back all the money that you borrowed from friends and family, and especially from the bank.

If you had this disorder for a long time, your list and amount of debt is likely to be high. Unless you are recently inheriting a fortune or winning the lottery, there is no way to pay back all the money in a short time.

Banks should be your first priority. You can transfer all your credits to one bank, i.e. loan from one bank with a low interest rate to pay back to all the other banks you owe to. This way, you can concentrate on one bank without having to split your money several ways.

A large amount of your wage, at least as much as you can afford, should go to this purpose. This way, unless you relapse and go back to shopping, you can pay back all that you owe the bank. The same technique can be applied to money borrowed from friends and relatives.

This is important: the large portion of your salary - except for the amount you need for rent, bills, fare and food – should go into paying back what you own.

It is important to maintain this strictly. It is very normal to become frustrated when a lot of your hard-earned money is going away without you having the chance to enjoy it. But this is absolutely necessary that you do not indulge and treat yourself too much and relapse without having to pay back what you owed.

Also, if you manage to pay back, and retain your old ways the moment you are free of credit, then the whole process has been a waste; you will be back where you started in no time.

Tip#7: Look for Alternatives

Shopping should no longer be the priority in your life. Instead, look for other activities you might be interested in. Go visit your extended family, go back to your childhood city, take up a new hobby, enroll into a language course, catch a movie, catch up with your reading, go for walks – in short, stay clear of malls and stores.

If you are on a tight budget having to pay back what you owe others, it may mean a lot of cutbacks on your lifestyle. But being on a budget doesn't mean you have to stop living your life. There can be a whole new range of healthier alternatives for you to choose from. Instead of hanging out with friends at the latest restaurants, hang out at home; instead of going to expensive dinners, have a potluck party; plan an inexpensive vacation to any of your friends' family homes instead of an exotic location; instead of gym, take up jogging.

Tip#8: Appoint a Guardian

The road to recovery is a tough road to travel alone and it will be best if you have a loved one along the way. This supportive person could be a spouse, a friend, a family member or even someone from the 'Shopaholics Anonymous (SA)' groups who will know the full extent of your problem, your full shopaholic history and help you recover. They will be your support at all the SA meetings you attend and the main person to throw you interventions. They should be given a right to scream at you when you are about to cross the lines of your budget or when you are close to relapsing.

It is a good idea to have someone who cares about you guide you through the way and hold you back when you need it.

When you know you have a problem with shopping and want to recover from it, self-help is indeed the best help there is. But if the recovery alone is proving to be difficult, it is advisable to take advice from your local SA about a counselor or a therapist to help you along the way.

Putting It All Together

I hope that you have found this book both helpful and informative in your quest to eliminate your shopping addiction.

The next step is for you to take action, implementing many of the suggestions found in this guide. Only through taking action and committing to it will you be able to curb your compulsive spending and buying habits. I understand your struggle, and know that you are strong enough and now have the tools necessary to change your life forever.

Good luck in your journey!

WAIT! Before You Leave…

Download the #1 Bestseller from Gamma Mouse Media for FREE! Hurry this offer won't last as it is for a limited time only. Reserve your free copy today at http://gammamouse.com.

A Special Gift for Our Readers!

Thank you so much for your purchase of this book. As a special gift for you we have included one of our bestselling Self-Improvement books: Procrastination: Triple Your Productivity and Accomplish Your Goals written by one of the most well-respected and influential experts on time management, Warren R. Sullivan.

I hope you enjoy!

Procrastination
Triple Your Productivity and Accomplish Your Goals

Warren R. Sullivan

Gamma Mouse
www.gammamouse.com

PROCRASTINATION
Copyright © 2014 by Warren R. Sullivan.
All rights reserved.

First Edition: April 2014
1234567890
A Gamma Mouse eBook
Published by Gamma Mouse, a dba of Xilytics, LLC.
www.gammamouse.com

This document is geared towards providing exact and reliable information in regards to the topic and issue covered. The publication is sold with the idea that the publisher is not required to render accounting, officially permitted, or otherwise, qualified services. If advice is necessary, legal or professional, a practiced individual in the profession should be ordered.

From a Declaration of Principles which was accepted and approved equally by a Committee of the American Bar Association and a Committee of Publishers and Associations.

In no way is it legal to reproduce, duplicate, or transmit any part of this document in either electronic means or in printed format. Recording of this publication is strictly prohibited and any storage of this document is not allowed unless with written permission from the publisher. All rights reserved.

The information provided herein is stated to be truthful and consistent, in that any liability, in terms of inattention or otherwise, by any usage or abuse of any policies, processes, or directions contained within is the solitary and utter responsibility of the recipient reader. Under no circumstances will any legal responsibility or blame be held against the publisher for any reparation, damages, or monetary loss due to the information herein, either directly or indirectly.

Respective authors own all copyrights not held by the publisher.

The information herein is offered for informational purposes solely, and is universal as so. The presentation of the information is without contract or any type of guarantee assurance.

The trademarks that are used are without any consent, and the publication of the trademark is without permission or backing by the trademark owner. All trademarks and brands within this book are for clarifying purposes only and are the owned by the owners themselves, not affiliated with this document.

Introduction

Procrastination. It has a drastic effect on productivity, on our ability to accomplish our goals in life. It can greatly impact our happiness, as we avoid doing something that we are dreading. Yet having to do it still hangs over our head.

Delaying something in order to often do something easier is an easy trap to fall into. Do it enough, and it suddenly becomes a habit. The problem with procrastination is we usually put off more important—but also more difficult—objectives for doing actions that are more trivial. For example, a college student might watch television rather than write a report.

Our time is valuable. It is the one thing that cannot be replaced, unlike money or objects. Yet it is wasted when we procrastinate. Saving this time should be our goal. We need to realize that our time would be better spend on accomplishing our most important objectives. When you have finished those, then reward yourself.

Stopping our procrastination is as easy as changing our attitude and stopping the habit that we have fallen into. In reading this guide, you will learn the tips and tricks necessary to stop procrastinating and start living. You don't have to suffer any longer, you can be happy and more productive, accomplishing all the important goals in your life quickly and easily. But you must take the first step and make a commitment to change yourself. Reading this book is a start, but if you don't act on what you learn change will not come. So consider this a call to action, a chance to truly change your life.

Getting to the root of the problem

Everyone procrastinates. It is part of being human. Whether because of laziness or not having the energy to tackle a difficult task, we choose to relax, to take the easy way out. Understand that not all procrastination should be viewed as bad. Often we need a break from the rigors of our day, a chance to get away from the stress of life. Some goals require great effort and energy to complete, so tackling them when you don't have much energy is realistic.

The line we don't want to cross is when we fool ourselves into believing that laziness is not having the energy to complete our task. Our first step is to recognize when we are being lazy. Clearly, we need to be honest with ourselves, we need to hold ourselves accountable. Secondly, we need to realize that time is our most valuable resource, and that it is finite. No one knows how much time they have, so it is essential to understand how important time is. When you sit down to watch television, recognize that this is time you will never get back.

To borrow a phrase from economics, understand that there is an opportunity cost to ever action you take. When you choose to do something, you lose the opportunity to use that time differently. When you make a choice, there is always a cost, remind yourself of this when you find yourself procrastinating. One of my methods for reminding myself to utilize every minute of my time as effectively as I can is to write the number 1440 on the white board in my office. This is the number of minutes in one day. Whenever I find myself procrastinating, I look at my board, and it helps me refocus on my task at hand.

People procrastinate for different reasons. The first step is to understand the reasoning behind our procrastinating. There may be more than one, but understanding the psychology behind our choices will help us effectively combat them, allowing us to change our faulty reasoning when it arises.

Cognitive distortions are a form of irrational thinking that often lead to procrastination. It is a magically type of thinking. Often we believe that we will be better equipped at some point in the future to handle our task, rather than completely the task at that time.

An example is a person who believes that they need to be in a certain mood in order to complete a task successfully. Or a person may believe that their motivation will increase in the future, and thus will be in a better position to accomplish their goals. Another one that happens in business quite frequently is an employee overestimating the time they have left to complete a task while also underestimating how long it will take them to do it.

If you are putting off a task, because you believe that you will be better suited in the future, realize that you are committing a fallacy. There is no evidence suggesting that your belief is true.

When we are confused about how to complete a task, and the details involved, we may procrastinate giving the reason that we need further instructions before we can continue. This allows us to set the project aside, until we find that we are butting up against a deadline. This reasoning often comes up with perfectionists who do not want to start a task until they are confident in their ability to complete it perfectly. To combat this reasoning, understand that completely the task initially to the best of your abilities and understanding, and then waiting for feedback is much more productive. It is easy to make corrections to your mistakes once the task is completed, as opposed to trying to do the task perfectly the first time. And there is always the possibility that the goal will be accomplished on your first attempt, without the need for further clarification. Don't fool yourself into thinking that if you have additional information, you will be better suited to complete the task. This is a cognitive distortion.

An offshoot of this is avoiding a task because you don't know how it should be done, that you require procedural information. Once again, this reasoning arises most often in the perfectionist, who believes they need to wait for the perfect situation in order to be successful. But look at the great inventors throughout history, who only through trial and error found out how to accomplish something amazing. Imagine if they had waited for the perfect moment, these inventions may never have come into existence. Remember that your goal is to accomplish your task, mistakes that you make can always be corrected. Don't fear failure. Instead, recognize it as an opportunity to learn.

I used to suffer from thinking I needed to take the time, to contemplate and reflect, before beginning a job. What I was doing was procrastinating, convincing myself I needed more information. This was clearly a logical fallacy. Thinking about the job was not going to make me more productive. What was going to make me more productive was doing it. If you believe you need more time to accomplish something, stop and examine whether that is true. Even if it is true, you can start the task now and revise it later as your thoughts begin to coalesce.

We have all had tasks that we had to do that we really didn't want to do. Income taxes come to mind. It is a responsibility, and sometimes that additional pressure makes a task unpleasant. And we are human, we do not want to do things we find unpleasant. We may even fool ourselves into thinking that there will be a point in the future when it will be easier to deal with an unpleasant task. Never make the mistake to think that a task that is unpleasant today will somehow miraculously improve in the future. It is always better to get the unpleasantness over immediately, rather than wait. I am reminded of my public speaking class in college. I always wanted to go first, and I could never understand why people wouldn't want to be first. Most found public speaking uncomfortable and unpleasant, but instead of immediately getting it out of the way and then relaxing, they chose to prolong how long the task would take them. Don't fall victim to this. If you find a task unpleasant, do it immediately; procrastination only makes it worse, and in the process makes you unhappy.

Now the opposite of procrastinating over tasks that we find unpleasant is to procrastinate over accomplishing goals that we don't care about. Finding the effort to complete a task when you are indifferent to the outcome is difficult. Often we may believe that we will feel more inclined to complete a task in the future when we feel more connected with the outcome. Usually indifference does not change, people don't suddenly start to care. These types of tasks often don't get tackled until we run up against a deadline. This can cause us additional stress as we must now take time to complete a task we don't care about instead of tasks that are much more important to us. Understand the cost of procrastinating may not be felt until the future when the task must be completed. Completing the task immediately saves you from future repercussions that you cannot anticipate.

I previously relayed the example of people believing that at some point in the future they will be in a better mood to accomplish a task. They may believe that certain moods make them more productive and believe that they need to wait for when they are in that mood. Recognize that this is an irrational reason you are giving yourself in order to procrastinate. While your emotions can affect your work, this is only generally in the case of extremes. Slight fluctuations in mood will have no effect, so don't convince yourself that you will be in a better mood to complete the task in the future. There is no truth to this.

A more specific example of this idea that a certain mood is essential for higher productivity is the case of individuals who wait until the last moment to start a task. The student who begins to study for mid-terms the night before the text, or the employee who starts an project the day before it is due are two examples of this. Waiting until the last minute to start because you think you are more productive up against a deadline is nothing more than believing that your mood makes you more productive at a point in the future. Don't fall for this procrastination excuse.

An additional reason you don't want to wait until you are up against a deadline is the cognitive distortion in which you overestimate the time you have while underestimating how long it will take you to accomplish a task. If you wait, believing you work better under pressure, you may place yourself in a situation in which you have significantly underestimated the time you will need. This may cause you to rush, resulting in sub-standard work. Or, even worse, you may miss your deadline completely. Avoid backing yourself into this corner where time works against you. Remember that we often believe that we have more time than we actually do.

Another reason people often give for procrastinating is that they had forgotten about a job. Often the reason that it was forgotten is intentional, the task may be unpleasant or one that we are indifferent about. If a deadline is far into the future, it can be easy to forget about our upcoming responsibilities. Or we may believe that we will get to it closer to the deadline. Understand that this is procrastination, and that there is nothing keeping you from completing the job now.

The final cognition distortion I will address is the belief that you don't want to currently complete a job because you are not feeling well, and that you will wait until you feel better. It should be evident how this is very similar to waiting for a specific mood in order to complete a task. Understand that there is no guarantee that you will feel better, in fact, you may end up feeling worse. Granted that people suffer from real health problems that greatly impact their ability to be productive. This is not what I am referring to. Instead, I refer to procrastinators who exaggerate how they feel to shirk their responsibilities. Don't be disingenuous with yourself about how you feel in order to avoid doing something.

Many of these cognition distortions are rooted in perfectionism or in our fear. We are either waiting for the moment to be right, or we are waiting to overcome our fear to do a task we may find unpleasant. Tell yourself that the moment will never be perfect, but it will be good enough to get the job done. Or if you are dealing with fear, realize that confronting your fear and doing the job now, will mean that once you have finished you will no longer have anything to fear. In fact, you will likely feel elated. This is a much better situation to be in than living under a cloud of dread.

Now that we have explored the underlying psychological reasons behind procrastination, our attention will turn to effective methods for dealing with procrastination. By employing the appropriate methods to our life, we will be able to become happier and more productive people.

Recognize the problem

Like with any addiction or problem, the first step is always to recognize and accept that you have a problem. Since you have purchased this book, I will assume that you have identified yourself as a procrastinator, and are now taking the proper steps to remedy this.

Do not feel shamed or embarrassed, identifying and attacking your problems is a noble and brave action. Focus on your self-awareness; stopping procrastination means keeping a keen eye on your behaviors. And making the necessary corrections.

Exercise

I want you to exam your behavior and thought processes. Write down three incidents in which you procrastinated.

Refer to the previous chapter if you want to show why your reasoning was faulty.

Find the root of the problem

Why are you procrastinating? Are you a perfectionist? Is fear keeping you from accomplishing certain tasks? Be honest with yourself. Discovering the root of your procrastination is important. If you recognize the cognition distortions that you are employing, this will give you a hint at the root of your procrastination. While knowing the underlying cause is helpful, identifying your faulty reasoning so you can correct it will have greater long-term gains.

If you are a perfectionist or if fear is holding you back, I want you to take a moment and examine your thinking. Why do you have to be perfect? Does it make you more productive? Does it make you happier? My guess is the answer will be "no". Tell yourself that accomplishing something perfectly is not the goal, the goal is only accomplishing your task. Withhold judgment, jobs are either done or not done. Also, ask yourself is it true that the longer you wait, the closer you will be to perfect? Or would you have done the same job either way? Does the evidence actually support your way of thinking?

The same approach can be taken if you suffer from fear. Ask yourself what you are afraid of? Most people fear a specific outcome. Is it rational to believe that outcome is guaranteed? I may fear dying in a plane crash, so I dread getting on a plane. But what are the chances that this event actually occurs. My chances are much greater of dying in a car accident on the way to the airport, but I don't have the same dread getting into a car. By nature, fear is not rational; it often arises from the fact that we have convinced ourselves of a terrible outcome, even though that outcome may be incredibly remote. Try to look at your fear rationally; assess the likelihood of the outcomes you fear. Then ask yourself: is it really that bad? Surprisingly, our fears are often overstated; they have a tendency to shrink when we look at them rationally.

Exercise

Using the previous chapter, identify any cognitive distortions you have fallen victim to. Can you discern what is behind this? If it is fear or the desire to be perfect, look at potential outcomes. Does it really need to be perfect? Is it a situation that you should be fearful of? Write down the reasons why you believe you need to be perfect, or write down why you should be afraid. Put it away for a day, and then read it again. Do your thoughts appear logical?

Prioritize with lists

Writing down a list is very effective in helping you achieve your goals. But you need to stick with it. Many people write lists, and then don't follow them. Remember the list is to help you stop procrastinating. Once you write the list, don't convince yourself out of following the order you set.

Put the jobs in order of priority, the most important being first and the least important being last. Estimate how long you believe each task will take you. Then multiply that time by a factor of three. Set this revised time as your deadline. The extra time will take into account the possibility that you are underestimating how long each task will take you; it serves as a buffer. The benefit is that if you complete your tasks early, you now have that extra time to do things you want to.

Keep your list close at hand. You can either write it down, or like I do, keep it on a mobile device.

There are numerous to-do list apps that will simplify the process.

Exercise

Write a list in which you prioritize your tasks by level of importance. Decide how long it will take you to do each task, then multiply that number by three. Write down the time needed next to each task on your list.

Divide and conquer

There are some tasks that are so large and unwieldy that estimating how long they will take is an incredibly difficult job. To help facilitate the process, break the large job into smaller segments. These segments should be small enough that you can estimate the time each one of them will take. Make certain you add in a buffer by multiplying each estimated time by three.

If you have a specific deadline, you can now add the time estimations for each of the smaller tasks to arrive at a figure for the entire project. This is a fantastic way to estimate large projects without placing yourself in a stressful situation as the deadline approaches. In fact, this approach is used quite frequently in the software industry for large multi-team projects.

Exercise

If you have a large project on your list, particularly if you are having difficulty estimating how long it will take, break it down into smaller segments. Now evaluate how much time each task will take, keeping the added buffer in mind.

Keep distractions to a minimum

One of the biggest productivity killers in recent years for businesses has been the Internet. It becomes easier for employees to procrastinate when they have other options that are more appealing only a mouse click away. With social media and email, there is always something new happening, and it can be quite difficult not to get immersed in this flow of constant information.

There are productivity plugins that will limit your access to the Internet by allowing you to stay online for short periods of time. If possible, I also recommend shutting down your email program, and only checking it at designated times. One method that is effective is to focus on your task for the first 50 minutes in the hour. In the remaining ten minutes, you can then check your email or Facebook status.

Additionally, a work or home environment can be distracting. People talking, a television playing, and other background noise can make you lose your focus. Listening to music through headphones or using earplugs is effective in blocking out distracting noise.

Exercise

Are you being distracted? Analyze your environment and decide whether you are being distracted. If you find yourself going online to check email or surf the Internet, try to use the 50 minute rule. Browser plugins will also limit your access to the Internet. Research, install, and configure them if you need this level of restriction.

If noise is a problem, buy earplugs or bring your headphones and MP3 player in order to listen to music.

Celebrate your accomplishments

You have completed your task list; time to celebrate. Giving yourself a reward after accomplishing your goals is wonderful way to encourage yourself to leave procrastination behind. The reward can be anything, an hour of television, a movie and dinner out, or an item you want. The point is to make it something you really desire, to properly give you a sense of accomplishment.

Exercise

Schedule a reward for yourself for completing your task list. Make it good. You deserve it.

Take care of yourself

Eating right and sleeping the recommended amount by your physician is essential in helping to reduce stress and anxiety. It is much easier to tackle your task list if you are feeling energized after a good night's sleep followed by a substantial breakfast. Often poor eating habits during the day lead to your blood sugar crashing in the afternoon, leaving you feeling sluggish and tired.

Make a point of eating a balanced diet spread over at least three meals over the course of the day. Maintain a regimented sleeping schedule. Try to go to bed and wake up at approximately the same time every day. Maintaining our sleep rhythms is very important.

Exercise, put it as a high priority on your task list if you have to. This can be as simple as taking a short walk. Exercising has the wonderful effect of increasing your energy, so take advantage.

Exercise

Evaluate your eating and sleeping habits, making the necessary changes. If you are not exercising, start. It can be as simple as a thirty minute walk per day.

Learn to say no

Many of us have the tendency to want to please other people. We take on more tasks and responsibilities than we have time for, causing us to have too many things to accomplish and not enough time to do them in. If you become too overwhelmed, there is a very good chance you will procrastinate rather than tackle your enormous list.

Learning to say no to task of low importance is key. When someone asks you to do something, look at what they are asking objectively. Is this task a high priority to you? What is the opportunity cost to you? Remember that your time is extremely valuable, it cannot be replaced. Time you spend on this task could be spent elsewhere. Unless it is a close family member, the most time I'm willing to spend on a task for someone is ten minutes. If I don't think I can accomplish it in ten minutes (after adding in my buffer), I will apologize and tell the person that I can't do it. Most people understand, they realize that we all lead busy lives. And if they don't, it is only further justification that I made the right decision.

Exercise

Look at your task list. Are there low priority jobs on it that you agreed to do for other people? If so, remove them from your list and let the person know, unless you believe you can accomplish it in a very short timeframe.

Be proactive in obtaining the information you need

During our examination of cognition distortions, we talked about procrastinating because we lack specific information about how to proceed or what our ultimate goal was. The way to avoid this problem is to always ask questions immediately on being given the task. Make certain you understand what your deliverables will be as well as the best way to proceed. There is no harm in asking and getting the answer. It will save you both time and aggravation.

With the advent of cellphones and email, people are generally accessible within a few hours. If the person you need to ask is not available, try to ask someone who has completed a similar task. Asking questions is not only an effective method for curtailing procrastination, it also has a generally positive affect on your life. We live in a society where the majority of people ask too few questions.

Exercise

Examine your task list. Is there a task that you have questions about? If so, contact the person who can answer your questions immediately. Even if it is late, send them an email. Don't wait, act on your questions right now.

Get into the habit

Procrastination is a bad habit, emphasis on habit. Habits need to be broken, and the best way to accomplish this is by replacing them with a new habit. If you have taken the suggested action to this point, you have already started on your way to replacing your habit to procrastinate. But it is only the start. Generally, it is believed that if a person can change their behavior for twenty-one days that change will become permanent.

Exercise

Find a calendar and mark off twenty-one days from today. Your goal is to keep up on doing your task list daily for the twenty-one days. Be aware that you will have to fight to keep procrastination from coming back in. Replacing old habits can be difficult, which means you need to remain vigilant of any back-sliding.

Make tasks relevant to you

Many of the jobs we do are done despite us being indifferent to the task or not enjoying it. The easiest way to combat this is to look at the task and accentuate a positive aspect of it. If you can find a good reason for doing something, it will make accomplishing it much more attractive to you. Think outside the box for reasons if you have to. Maybe completing a task will open up a new opportunity in your life, or allow you to connect with different people. Accomplishing it may give you the opportunity to make new friends.

There are a variety of reasons why a task should be completed. You need to find the one that holds the most appeal to you.

Exercise

Take a moment to examine your list. Are there any jobs you do not enjoy to do? Are there any tasks you feel indifferent about? If so, think of a good reason, one that appeals to you, of what completing the task could mean for you. Try to find a reason that makes you want to tackle the job.

Conclusion

I hope that you have found this journey helpful. If you have participated in the recommended exercises along the way, you should be commended. You have clearly decided you want to change, and that is a huge first step to becoming a more productive person.

Procrastination is not something you need to suffer with, the answers are all right here in this guide. Understand that procrastination can have deep psychological roots, causes that take time and effort to overcome. The best way to accomplish this is to face it head on. If you are a perfectionist, try completing a task even though you may not feel it is perfect, or up to your usual standards. If fear is holding you back, stand up to it by imagining the worst outcome, and then honestly evaluating how likely that outcome will come to be.

Humans suffer from many irrational thoughts, convinced of the truth of an idea even though the evidence suggests the opposite. Recognizing these irrational thoughts is the first step in dispelling them. Once you realize you are being illogical, the thought fails to hold any power over you anymore. Never take anything for granted, continuously question your thoughts, assessing them for validity. This isn't only the key to stopping procrastination, it also leads to a life that is happier and more productive.

I wish you all the success in your journey.

WAIT! Before You Leave…

Download the #1 Bestseller from Gamma Mouse Media for FREE! Hurry this offer won't last as it is for a limited time only. Reserve your free copy today at http://gammamouse.com.

Now Available From Gamma Mouse

Below you will find other popular Amazon bestsellers from Gamma Mouse.

A Beginner's Guide to Parkour – Jeff Boyer

Apple Cider Vinegar – Kelsey Gannon

Bedwetting – Nicole Harrington

Body Lotions – Sophia Rocha

Brain Training Boot Camp – Warren R. Sullivan

Cellulite Reduction – Emily V. Steinhauser

Compulsive Hoarding – Emily V. Steinhauser

Eliminate Acne – Anne D. Spellman

Essential Oils – Emily V. Steinhauser

Forex Indicators – Warren R. Sullivan

Get Healthy with Essential Oils – Alicia Martinez

How to Make Money on Fiverr Secrets Revealed – James Chen

How to Reduce Cellulite – Anne D. Spellman

Kindle Publishing Secrets Revealed – James Chen

Knee Pain Treatment – Emily V. Steinhauser

Lust for Me – Amelia Austin

Marriage Problems – Emily V. Steinhauser

Memory Enhancement – Warren R. Sullivan

Mutual Funds – James Chen

Natural Oils – Nicole Harrington

Paleo Diet Unleashed – Jeff Boyer

Procrastination – Warren R. Sullivan

Puppy Training – Zach Rucker

Quiet – Amelia Austin

Reiki – Sophia Rocha

Relieve Your Knee Pain – Alicia Martinez

Speed Reading Training – Warren R. Sullivan

Stop Shopping Addiction – Lindsay Sullivan

The Quick Start Guide to Macarons – Lindsay Stotts

The Quick Start Guide to Perfect Pancakes – Lindsay Stotts

Printed in Poland
by Amazon Fulfillment
Poland Sp. z o.o., Wrocław